# The Cube

Anne Taylor

Seed Learning

## Top Phonics Readers 3
### The Cube

Anne Taylor

Acquisitions Editor: Rose Morgan
Content Editor: Liana Robinson
Illustrators: Story 1 - Genie Espinosa; Story 2 - Jillian Altmeyer;
            Story 3 - Conor Rawson; Story 4 - Celeste Gagnon
Design: Highline Studio

http://www.seed-learning.com

ISBN: 978-1-9464-5275-7

10 9 8 7 6 5 4 3 2 1
21 20 19 18 17

# Contents

# The Red Cake

-ate, -ake, -ame,
-ape, -ave, -ane

Written by **Anne Taylor**

Illustrated by **Genie Espinosa**

Today's the date!
Mom! Dad! Today's the date!

Let's b**ake** a c**ake**!
Let's m**ake** it big!
Let's m**ake** it red!

It's good!
We put a wave on it.
We put a name on it.

We put the cake in a box.
We put tape on it.
We make the box red, too.

"Dan, get your cape.
Jake, get your mane."
Uh, oh! Jake hates his mane.

We open the gate.
We go on the lane.
We go to the lake.

Grandpa! We have a cake.
It's for you!
Happy birthday!

# Ready to Ride

-ide, -ike, -ime, -ine,
-ipe, -ire, -ite, -ive

Written by **Anne Taylor**
Illustrated by **Jillian Altmeyer**

Lucy is nine.
She likes to ride her bike.
It's a red bike.

Lucy rides her bike with her family.
They ride to the vines.

There they hike.
They hike to a lake.
They all dive into the lake.

They have lime juice.
Yum!
Then they fly a kite.

They make a fire.
It's nice by the lake.

They had a good time!
But look at their bikes.
Look at the tires!

Lucy wipes her bike.
Now it's ready to ride again.

# A Home for a Mole

## -ome, -ole, -one, -ope, -ose, -ote

Written by **Anne Taylor**

Illustrated by **Conor Rawson**

"Hello, Mike Mole," says Dave Mole.
"I got your note."
"Hello, Dave Mole," says Mike Mole.
"I hope you are well."

"Let's go to my home," says Mike Mole.
"My home is a hole."

"A hole?" says Dave Mole.
"My home is a dome. Let's go to my home."

"But I love my home," says Mike Mole.
"I have a bone in my hole."

"A bone? I have a pole with a rope," says Dave Mole.

"And I have a hose and a rose,"
says Mike Mole.
"Me, too!" says Dave Mole.

"We love our homes. Your hole is nice.
My dome is nice. Now, let's have a cone!"

# The Cube

**-ube, -ule, -une,
-ure, -use, -ute**

Written by **Anne Taylor**
Illustrated by **Celeste Gagnon**

What can we do with this cube?
Let's use it for a game.
A cube game!

It is a dune.
No, it is a mule.
We can ride it!

What can we do with this tube?
Let's use it for a new game.
A tube game!

I see an elephant with a lute.
The elephant is playing a tune!

I see a cute cat.
The cat has a prune!

What can we do with this lure?
I know!

Let's use it to catch my cat!
Ha ha ha!

# Word List

Story 1

bake

cake

Jake

lake

make

name

lane

mane

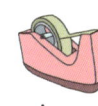
cape

tape

date

gate

hate

wave

Story 2

ride

bike

hike

lime

time

nine

vine

wipe

fire

tire

kite

dive

# Word List

## Story 3

hole

mole

pole

dome

home

bone

cone

hope

rope

hose

rose

note

## Story 4

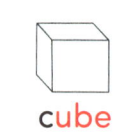
cube

tube

mule

dune

prune

tune

lure

use

cute

lute

# How to Use

The following are some ideas for ways to use the stories in this book.

## Idea 1

- ★ Choose a story.
- ★ Look at the **Word List** for that story.
- ★ Find each word from the list in the story.
- ★ Then read the story.

## Idea 2

- ★ Choose a story.
- ★ Look at the illustrations for the story.
- ★ Talk about the illustrations: Point and say the words you know in the illustrations.
- ★ Look for the words from the illustrations in the story while you read.

## Idea 3

- ★ Choose a story.
- ★ Look at all the words with red letters in the story. Circle the words you know.
- ★ If you don't know a word, check the **Word List**.
- ★ Then read the story.
- ★ After reading, look at the words again. Can you remember the meaning of each one?

## Idea 4

- ★ Choose a story.
- ★ Look at the illustration on each page: What do you see? What is happening?
- ★ Guess what you think the page will say.
- ★ Then read the page.
- ★ Repeat for every page of the story.